LifeTimes

The Story of Nelson Mandela

by James Riordan
illustrated by Neil Reed

Belitha Press

First published in the UK in 2001 by

Belitha Press Ltd
London House, Great London Wharf
Parkgate Road, London SW11 4NQ

Produced for Belitha Press by
White-Thomson Publishing Ltd
2/3 St Andrew's Place
Lewes, BN7 1UP

ISBN 1 84138 343 0

British Library Cataloguing in Publication Data for this book is available
from the British Library.

Editor: Steve White-Thomson
Designer: Simon Borrough
Language consultant: Norah Granger, Senior Lecturer in Primary Education
  at the University of Brighton.

With thanks to Kay Barnham for her editorial help in the latter stages
of this book.

Printed in China

Introduction

This story takes place in South Africa,
a country rich in gold and diamonds and
home to black and white Africans.

South Africa's apartheid policy of white
rule reserved the best land and jobs for whites.

But black and coloured (mixed race)
Africans began to fight for their rights.
One of their leaders was a young black
lawyer called Nelson Mandela…

Sharpeville

Mary was nine years old. She lived in the little town of Sharpeville, South Africa. Today was a special day.

'Put on your Sunday frock, Mary,' said Mum, fussing about like a mother hen.

Dad's deep voice rang out. 'We're just going to look, not take part. You know I don't hold with breaking the law. We're not looking for trouble like some hotheads.'

'That's not fair, Dad,' said Mary's brother, David. 'They're going peacefully to the police station — to protest against the pass laws.'

At half-past one Mary and her family set off
towards the police station. It seemed that half
the town was going to see the fun.

The day was hot, the mud track hard and
dusty, the sky a gentle blue. The mood was
happy, as if they were on a church outing.

They sat down on the grass near the police
gates, singing hymns to pass the time.

At two o'clock, six young men linked arms and started walking towards the gates of the police station, chanting, 'No Pass! No Pass!'

All at once, a long line of policemen came into the yard. They were pointing their guns at the young men.

No one expected what happened next.

With no warning, the police opened fire.

There were no shots in the air, just a hail
of bullets aimed right into the crowd.

There was panic. The air was thick with
screams and groans, everyone running for their
lives. People were crying out, 'Help me!'

Mum was the first to fall. As Dad stopped
to help her, he shooed Mary and David on.

'Run, run for cover!' he shouted.

Those were their father's last words, before he, like the others, was shot in the back. He, too, fell to the ground and lay in the dust, one arm spread over his dying wife.

South Africa had been under white rule since the seventeenth century, during which time the whites had made many laws – the most hated of these were the pass laws. An African needed a pass to get a job, to travel and to be out after dark. On 21 March 1960, the Sharpeville protest took place to demonstrate against the pass laws – 69 people were shot dead and more than 400 wounded. The killings shook the world.

Burn Your Passes!

The day after the Sharpeville killings, four men met in nearby Johannesburg. They were members of the ANC, the political party fighting for African rights.

'We can't stand by while the police shoot people in cold blood,' Joe was saying. 'It's time to fight back – with guns and bombs.'

'No,' insisted Nelson Mandela, 'No violence.'

'What if we ask Africans to burn their passes instead?' suggested Walter Sisulu.

'And give them a chance to mourn for the dead,' added Duma.

It was agreed. The message went out.

A few days later, the major cities came to
a standstill, while funerals were held.

Then Mandela and others led the way by
burning their passes in public. It was a challenge
to white rule – a challenge that the police
were quick to answer.

In the early hours of the next morning,
Nelson Mandela was woken by a loud noise.
Six white policemen burst in and turned the
house upside-down, before handcuffing him.

'You're a dangerous troublemaker, Mandela,'
they told him. 'We're going to shut your
mouth – for good.'

Winnie, Mandela's wife, stood helpless.
His two little daughters, Zenani and Zindzi,
were crying. They held tightly to their father's
hands in the strange iron handcuffs.

'Where are you taking him?' Winnie asked. The police refused to say.

'Don't worry,' Nelson told his wife and daughters. 'I'll be home very soon.'

They watched the police cars drive off into the dark night. Would they ever see him again?

When the Afrikaner National Party came to power in 1948, they made apartheid more harsh. The party believed themselves to be chosen by God to rule over blacks. Their cruel laws shocked many people abroad. The African National Congress (ANC) started to fight back.

Prison

Nelson soon found himself in a prison yard
with 40 other prisoners. They too had been
dragged from their beds.

The next morning, they were pushed into
a stinking cell. The toilet was just a hole in the
floor – and it was blocked. The prisoners had
no food, no blankets and nowhere to sit.

As the hours went by, more and more men were squeezed into the small cell. It became unbearable.

'Next time they open the door,' said Nelson, 'run out into the yard. We won't return until we're fed.'

When the door swung open again, the prisoners rushed out. The guard was furious.

'Get back or I'll crack open your skulls!' he bawled. After Sharpeville, they knew that this was no empty threat.

But the men stood firm. The station chief
was called. 'Take your hands out of your
pockets!' he shouted at Mandela. 'Show respect.'

Nelson kept his hands in his pockets.

'I will – when you show us respect,' he replied.
'We want food.'

The chief stormed off.

Several hours later, when the men were back in their cell, a guard brought them a pot of cold corn porridge. No bowls or spoons. They had to dip their hands in the pot to eat.

Later they were given blankets – thick with dried blood and vomit, and crawling with fleas.

Next day, Nelson was taken in front of the station chief. 'Boy, you are cheeky,' he said.

'I am 42 years old. I am a man,' replied Nelson. 'My name is Mr Mandela.'

Nelson stared the chief straight in the eye.

The chief jumped up. He would knock some respect into this cheeky black boy!

But just at that moment a message arrived: *Send Mandela to Pretoria. He is wanted for treason.*

Out of the frying pan, into the fire…

Nelson Mandela, who had trained as a lawyer, helped to turn the ANC into a mass freedom movement. They got together with other anti-apartheid groups, such as the Communist Party and the Indian Congress. The ANC believed in non-violent action – boycotts, strikes, civil disobedience and non-cooperation with the white government. In June 1955, the anti-apartheid groups issued a Freedom Charter setting out their aims. Soon after, the police arrested the leaders on a charge of high treason.

No Easy Walk

Later that day, Nelson was pushed into a filthy prison cell in the capital city, Pretoria. He was to stay here for the next 14 months.

It wasn't until the end of March 1961 that he stood in the dock, awaiting his fate. He knew that if he were found guilty of treason, he would receive the death penalty. The white judge asked if he had anything to say.

'My Lord,' said the prisoner, 'there is no easy walk to freedom. We Africans know that our struggle brings great suffering. But we choose that way because we prize freedom above all else.'

'But, isn't your freedom a threat to whites?' asked the judge.

'We are not fighting whites,' replied Mandela. 'We are against white rule. Some whites support us in this fight. We want votes for all, white and black alike. Let us live together in peace and freedom.'

The judge gave his verdict.

'Not guilty. You may go.'

Outside the court Nelson was greeted by a cheering, dancing crowd. Together they sang 'Nkosi Sikelel iAfrika' (God Bless Africa), the song of the freedom movement.

But, although Nelson was free, the judge had banned him from writing or speaking in public. This was something he could not accept.

So he hugged his wife and daughters to him. 'I must go away,' he said. 'Maybe for a long time.

There comes a time when a man has to live the life of an outlaw.'

'Don't you love us any more?' cried little Zenani, bursting into tears.

Her words pierced his heart. 'I love you dearly,' he said quietly. 'What I do is for you and millions of children like you. I want you to live in freedom.' At the door, he kissed Winnie and the two girls, then slid into a waiting car.

South Africa's apartheid laws divided the country's people into four main groups: whites (18 per cent of the population), Africans (70 per cent), Indians (3 per cent) and coloureds or people of mixed race (9 per cent). In jail they were held in different cells and fed differently: whites received white bread and sugar; Indians and coloureds had brown bread and sugar; Africans had no bread and no sugar.

The Car Repair Man

Now began the life of a hunted man. Secretly, Mandela went all over the country, leading the freedom struggle.

It wasn't easy for a tall, well-known man to disguise himself. He grew a beard, wore torn and greasy overalls and spoke in a slow, husky voice. One day he was a window cleaner, the next a taxi driver; he became an errand boy, a student, even the boxer he had once been.

One day, when Winnie was at work, she received a phone call. 'You need your car mended, ma'am?' asked the caller.

'Yes, I do.'

'Drive to the corner of Smuts Avenue,' said the voice. 'Our man will meet you there.'

Winnie went at once, hoping the man might have a message from Nelson. A tall, bearded man in blue overalls met her at the corner.

'Sit in the back,' he said roughly.

As he drove off, she whispered, 'How is my husband?'

'Nelson? Oh, he's fine. Misses his wife and family though.'

'Can you get a message to him? Can you tell him that we miss him badly and love him for what he's doing?'

For a minute the man was silent. Then, as he pulled up at a garage, he looked round. With a big smile, he said, 'Why don't you tell him yourself?'

Winnie stared in amazement. It was Nelson!

After they'd talked for a while, he drove back to the city centre, halting at a stop sign.

'Goodbye, Winnie,' he said simply. He got out and vanished into the crowd.

During Nelson's time on the run, he had many narrow escapes, once climbing down a rope from a high flat to make his get-away. Yet all the time he popped up at rallies, wrote leaflets and even gave television interviews.

The police were desperate. They put many thousands of people in jail and banned all meetings and leaflets. But, for 17 months, they just couldn't catch Nelson Mandela.

While he was free, the ANC asked Nelson to form a new organization: *Umkhonto we Sizwe* (Spear of the Nation). This signalled a big change in tactics: from non-violent protest to sabotage – blowing up power stations, railway and telephone lines. 'The time has come to hit back in defence of our people and of freedom,' wrote Mandela.

Robben Island

At last, the police caught Mandela.

He was sentenced to life imprisonment on Robben Island and arrived there just after his 46th birthday. This was to be his home for the next 24 years.

The rocky island had its own wild beauty. Covered in yellow bushes and sweet-smelling eucalyptus trees, it was home to deer and ostrich, seals and penguins.

In winter, the island was damp and bitterly cold, with thick mist rolling in off the South Atlantic Ocean. But on a clear day, prisoners could see Table Mountain on the mainland, and ships sailing to and from Cape Town, just 10 kilometres away.

So near, yet so far.

Nelson's cell was tiny. On the stone floor was a mat and bedroll. In winter, his khaki shorts and shirt, thin jumper and jacket could not keep out the cold. Before sunrise each day, the guards woke him for a cold wash and he cleaned out his toilet bucket.

He tried to keep his dignity. On the first day, he was marched off to work with the other prisoners. 'Faster! Faster!' yelled the guards. But he walked slowly, and struck up a freedom song. Other men joined him in the song.

There was nothing the guards could do.

Work meant digging up and breaking large stone slabs. The prisoners worked all day long, come rain or shine. Their arms and backs ached, their feet and hands were covered in blisters, their eyes were red and full of grit. At the end of the day, the prisoners looked more like ghosts than human beings, covered in thick, white dust.

But no matter how tired they were, they would sing together from their cells, replying to Mandela's shout of, '*Amandla!*' (power), with the word '*Ngawethu!*' (to the people).

Once every six months, Nelson was allowed one visit of 30 minutes and one letter of no more than 500 words. No children were allowed, so Winnie came alone.

She could only see her husband through a small window, and hear him via a telephone. They were only allowed to talk about their family, and in English, so that the guards could understand what they were saying.

Back home, Winnie told the children all about the father they hadn't seen for years – and were not to see for many more.

The ANC continued its campaign of sabotage and the government stepped up its terror. In July 1967, the ANC President Albert Lutuli was run down and killed. Nelson's wife Winnie was beaten up, her house burnt down and then she was put in jail. Steve Biko, the black student leader, was tortured to death. His close friend, Ahmed Timol, 'fell' to his death from the tenth floor of a police headquarters.

Zindzi's Story

Soon after Zindzi's 16th birthday, she went with her sister Zeni to Robben Island. Their mother had warned them not to cry, saying, 'It only makes the guards happy!'

The only passengers to board the ferry in Cape Town docks were the two girls in their grey school dresses, and a crowd of white prison guards singing rugby songs.

At the prison, they were shown into a tiny room with a window in one wall. The girls sat on a bench with guards on either side of them. What would their father look like after 12 years? He was nearly 60 years old.

Suddenly, there he was behind the window. They picked up the phone.

'My, my, how grown up you girls are,' Nelson said with a smile. 'You're too big to sit on my lap now. Well, how do I look?'

'Different. You used to be big and fat,' Zindzi said quietly.

'I'm on a diet,' he said jokingly. 'I'm in training to be a boxing champion.'

A guard broke in: 'Talk only about family!'

'What does your teacher say?' Dad asked.

'Oh… right now she's on a trip,' replied Zeni. 'But she's really fine, says we're doing well at our lessons.'

'And what's the news from church?' asked Dad. 'I hear there's a new vicar.'

'Church is fuller than ever,' said Zindzi. 'The new vicar is spreading the word abroad.'

Mum had explained the code they were to use to fool the guards. She was 'teacher'. Being on a 'trip' meant that she'd been sent away by the police.

The 'church' was the ANC, and the new vicar was its leader Oliver Tambo. To avoid jail, he worked outside the country.

'Time's up!' yelled a guard.

The girls wanted to kiss the glass, but a guard blocked their way. They watched sadly as Nelson was led away, whispering, 'Bye, Dad.'

It was very hard not to cry.

The year that Zindzi was 16, and old enough to visit her father, a shocking event occurred. On 16 June 1976, as a crowd of black schoolchildren protested in Soweto near Johannesburg, many were shot dead. More and more people all over the world began to protest against apartheid laws. They boycotted South African goods, ran on to sports grounds to stop white South African teams from playing and banned the country from the Olympic Games.

I Just Called to Say...

Years passed. Soon Nelson Mandela would
be 70 years old, and in his 24th year in jail.
By this time, the cry of 'Free Mandela!' was
sounding round the world. He had become the
best-known symbol of the fight for freedom.

To mark Mandela's 70th birthday, a huge
open-air concert was held in London.
Millions watched on TV.

The blind American singer Stevie Wonder came on stage holding a telephone. 'Friends,' he said, 'do you love Nelson?'

A great roar echoed round the stadium. 'Shall we wish him Happy Birthday?'

He dialled a number. A hush came over the vast crowd. Would he really get through to Nelson Mandela on faraway Robben Island?

'Nelson?' said Stevie Wonder. 'Happy Birthday to you. We have a message for you.' He held the phone towards the crowd and everyone burst into song:
'I just called to say I love you, I just called to say how much I care.'

At home and abroad people wanted change so much, that two years later, the white government of South Africa had to give in.

It was a hot summer's day in the Cape.

A large crowd was waiting outside Verster Prison, where Mandela was now held. The world was waiting for Mandela to emerge. What would he look like? No pictures of him had been allowed for nearly 30 years.

Then, a shout went up: 'He's coming! He's coming!'

Through the prison gates came a tall, slim, grey-haired man in a smart suit. He was walking hand-in-hand with Winnie.

All along the road to Cape Town, black and white people sang together and danced with joy as the car carrying Nelson and Winnie slowly drove past.

At City Hall, Nelson Mandela came on to the balcony, raised his fist in salute and cried out to the crowd, 'Mayibuye iAfrika!'

May Africa return!

Although Mandela was freed in February 1990, the fight was not yet won. Apartheid was shaken, but not defeated. It took four more years of struggle before, finally, the government agreed to elections. For the first time Africans, Indians and coloured people were allowed to vote. The ANC won the right to run the country.

The Rainbow Nation

On 10 May 1994, thousands of cheering people stood outside Parliament in the capital city Pretoria. They had come to greet South Africa's new President.

In the waiting crowd was a 43-year-old woman from Sharpeville. Her name was Mary. She had been waiting ten hours.

'Aren't you tired?' someone asked.

'I've been waiting 34 years,' she replied with a smile. 'I don't mind waiting a little longer. I only wish Mum and Dad could have lived to see this day.'

Finally, to a roar of welcome, President
Nelson Mandela, with his daughters Zenani
and Zindzi, mounted the stand. The new flag
was slowly raised. It showed the old and the
new: the ANC black for the people, green for
the land and yellow for the gold, with the old
red, white and blue.

Members of the new Parliament were there
to represent the new Rainbow Nation, the
nation of many colours. Now, there were black
and brown and white men, and 106 women.
Everyone wore colourful clothes of all kinds
– rich saris, tribal robes and smart suits.

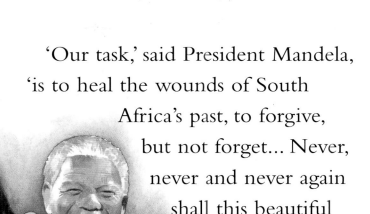

'Our task,' said President Mandela, 'is to heal the wounds of South Africa's past, to forgive, but not forget... Never, never and never again shall this beautiful land see the oppression of one by another.' Mary from Sharpeville nodded through her tears.

President Mandela saw the new South Africa through its first difficult years. Then he handed over to his friend Thabo Mbeki. Despite Mandela's long years in prison, he worked tirelessly to heal the wounds of South Africa's past. He even went to Robben Island to meet and forgive his former guards. He was 82 in the year 2000. At last he was able to find peace, living in a small cottage near his birthplace, surrounded by his many grandchildren.

Apartheid

Under the apartheid system, Africans, Indians and coloureds (mixed race) were treated as a lower class. Although they made up 82 per cent of the population, they were given only 13 per cent of the land. They could not use schools, universities, libraries, beaches, parks, theatres, restaurants or even toilets reserved for whites.

Non-whites were not allowed to play for or against teams with white players. When England included a non-white player in their cricket team to tour South Africa, the visit was cancelled.

It was against the law for a white man to have a non-white girlfriend and no mixed marriages were permitted.

Africans, Indians and coloureds were not allowed to vote.

In 1993, Nelson Mandela accepted the Nobel Peace Prize on behalf of all those who worked for peace and stood against racism.

Timeline

1918	18 July	Nelson Rolihlahla Mandela is born.
1944	April	He helps to set up the African National Congress Youth League.
1948		Afrikaner National Party takes power and introduces its apartheid policy.
1952		Mandela qualifies as a lawyer.
1955		By the Bantustan (Homelands) law, whites are given 87 per cent of land.
1956	5 December	Mandela is charged with treason.
1958	June	Mandela marries Winnie Madikizela.
1960	21 March	Police shoot 69 dead in Sharpeville.
1961	March	Mandela, freed from jail, leads freedom struggle as an outlaw.
1964		Mandela is sentenced to life imprisonment on Robben Island.
1976	16 June	Many children shot dead in Soweto.
1978–81		The 'Free Mandela' campaign spreads across the world.
1988	July	A large concert is held in London to mark Mandela's 70th birthday.
1990	11 February	Mandela is finally freed after 27 years.
1993	February	De Klerk's white government agrees to elections.
1994	4 May	ANC wins elections.
1994	10 May	Mandela becomes President of South Africa.
1999	June	Mandela retires from public life.

More information

Books to read

Nelson Mandela by Sean Connolly, Heinemann 2000.

Long Walk to Freedom by Nelson Mandela, Abacus 1995.

Nelson Mandela, The Man and the Movement by Mary Benson, Penguin 1994.

Nelson Mandela by Richard Killeen, Wayland 1995.

Nelson Mandela by Hakim Adi, Hodder/Wayland 2000.

Websites

http://www.mandela-tribute.com/index2.html

http://www.nmcf.co.za/

http://www.pbs.org/wgbh/pages/frontline/shows/mandela/

Glossary

Afrikaner National Party (ANP) The party of the Dutch-speaking people of South Africa.

African National Congress (ANC) A political party led by black Africans.

apartheid White rule over non-whites; racist policy officially introduced in 1948.

coloured Someone of mixed (white and black) background.

oppression Keeping people down by cruel methods.

pass laws Laws forcing Africans to carry passes that controlled their lives.

sabotage To deliberately damage or destroy property.

segregation Keeping people of a different colour apart.

treason (high treason) Intending to overthrow the government.

Index